W9-CKE-450

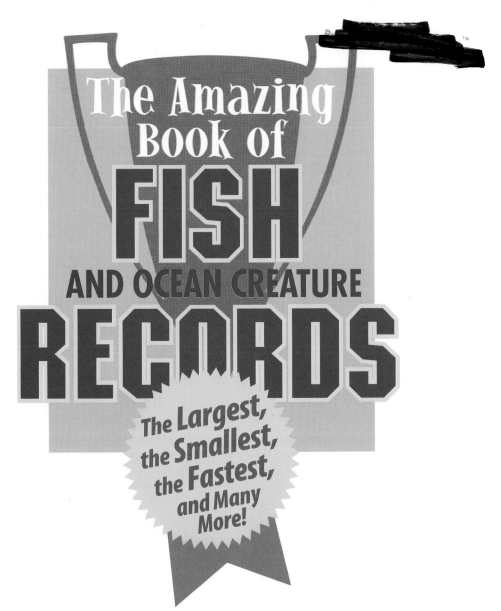

The Amazing Book of FISH AND OCEAN CREATURE RECORDS

The Largest, the Smallest, the Fastest, and Many More!

By Samuel G. Woods

Illustrations by Jeff Cline

BLACKBIRCH PRESS, INC.

WOODBRIDGE, CONNECTICUT

For Nathan and Emma, my two favorite guppies.
–SGW

Published by Blackbirch Press, Inc.
260 Amity Road
Woodbridge, CT 06525
web site: http://www.blackbirch.com
e-mail: staff@blackbirch.com

© 2000 Blackbirch Press, Inc.
First Edition

Printed in China

10 9 8 7 6 5 4 3 2 1

Library of Congress Cataloging-in-Publication Data
Woods, Samuel G.
    The amazing book of fish and ocean creature records: the largest, the smallest, the fastest, and many more! / by Samuel G. Woods; illustrations by Jeff Cline.
        p. cm.
    Includes index.
    ISBN 1-56711-370-2
    1. Fishes—Miscellanea—Juvenile literature. 2. Marine animals—Miscellanea—Juvenile literature. [1. Fishes—Miscellanea. 2. Marine animals—Miscellanea 3. Questions and answers.] I. Cline, Jeff, ill. II. Title

QL617.2.W66 2000
597—dc21   00-034245

Contents

• • • • • • • •

What's the LARGEST Fish?

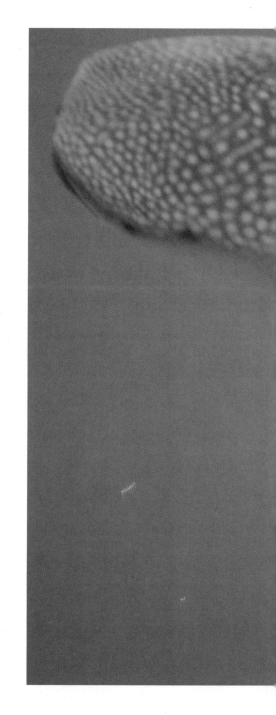

The Whale Shark

Some whale sharks can grow longer than 60 feet (18 m)—more than twice the length of a basketball court—and can weigh more than 50,000 pounds (22,680 kg)!

NOTEPAD

This gigantic fish looks fierce but is really quite harmless. Its small teeth and slow movement pose little threat to most creatures in the ocean. Whale sharks are found in tropical waters, where they feed mostly on plankton and small fishes. These huge animals like to swim near the water's surface and be a hazard to nearby ships. Because they cannot move very fast, whale sharks are often unable to avoid a swiftly approaching vessel.

Whale sharks look dangerous, but they are really slow-moving, gentle creatures.

What's the SMALLEST Fish?

The Pygmy Goby

The average pygmy goby is less than 1/2 inch (1.7 cm) long. That's about the size of a pencil eraser!

Pygmy gobies
spend more time
than most fish
raising their
young.

NOTEPAD

Pygmy gobies are found mostly in tropical coral reefs. After laying their eggs, gobies attach them to the reef and care for them until they hatch. This sort of parental care is unusual for fish. After the young hatch, goby parents will sometimes even care for their young for a short time. There are about 600 species of gobies around the world.

What's the FASTEST Fish?

The Sailfish

At top speed, a sailfish can swim nearly 70 miles (113 km) per hour!

Sailfishes are large, powerful swimmers that can grow to 7 feet (2.1m) long.

NOTEPAD

These large, open-ocean fishes use their dorsal fins to cut through the water at top speeds. Feeding mostly on squid and mid-sized surface fishes, sailfishes grow very quickly. The average length of a year-old fish is 4 to 5 feet (1.2 to 1.5 m). Full grown, an adult can be 7 feet (2.1 m) long and can weigh nearly 120 pounds (54 kg).

What's the LARGEST CRUSTACEAN?

The Giant Spider Crab

The largest spider crab ever reported weighed 14 pounds (6.4 kg) and had a claw span of 12 feet (3.7 m)! That's the length of 2 average human adult males!

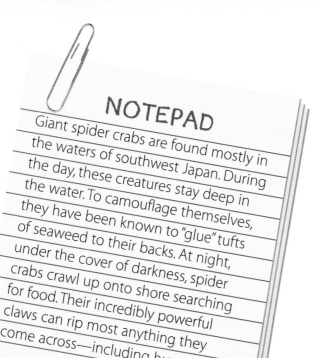

NOTEPAD

Giant spider crabs are found mostly in the waters of southwest Japan. During the day, these creatures stay deep in the water. To camouflage themselves, they have been known to "glue" tufts of seaweed to their backs. At night, under the cover of darkness, spider crabs crawl up onto shore searching for food. Their incredibly powerful claws can rip most anything they come across—including human flesh.

Giant spider crabs are found mostly in the waters of southwest Japan.

Which SHELLFISH Has the LARGEST SHELL?

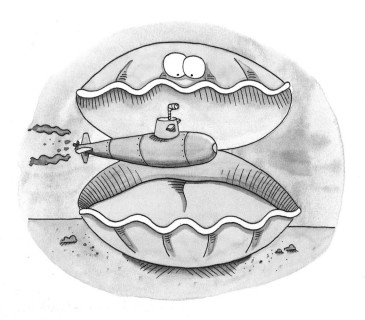

The Giant Clam

A full-grown giant clam can grow to 4 feet (1.2 m) in length and can weigh more than 500 pounds (227 kg)!

The giant clam is found in the Indian and Pacific oceans.

NOTEPAD

Giant clams are by far the largest of all the clam species. These shellfish can be found in the shallow coral reefs of the southern Indian and Pacific oceans. The clam's super-large shell provides a home for many smaller animal species. The outer surface of the shell may be covered with corals, small shellfish, sponges, and other clams. Aborigines of Australia eat the meat of the giant clam and use the shells as washtubs for their children!

What's the LARGEST MOLLUSK?

* * * * * * * * * *

The Giant Squid

A fully grown adult giant squid can weigh more than 3,000 pounds (1,361 kg)! That's roughly the weight of a small sport utility vehicle!

NOTEPAD

Giant squid are found mostly in the freezing depths of the Arctic Ocean. There, deep in the water, they hunt for fish. When prey is captured, it is placed in the squid's mouth. From there, a throat covered by a rough, file-like organ—called a radula—forces the food down the esophagus (throat passage). A squid's esophagus passes directly through its brain on its way to its stomach!

Giant squid eat medium-sized fish in the Arctic Ocean.

Which Fish Species Has MALES THAT "GIVE BIRTH"?

The Sea Horse

A male sea horse gets eggs from a female, fertilizes them in his pouch, and then incubates them until they hatch!

Sea horses are members of the pipefish family.

NOTEPAD

Sea horses are members of the pipefish family. They are found mostly in temperate (fairly-warm) and tropical (warm) waters. To reproduce, a female sea horse will deposit about 100 eggs into a pouch on the male's abdomen. The male then releases sperm into the pouch, which fertilizes the eggs. The embryos develop for the next 2 to 6 weeks. When the young emerge from their father's body, it looks just like he is "giving birth!"

What's the LONGEST-LIVED MOLLUSK?

The Quahog (marine clam)

Quahogs can live to be 200 years old! In fact, these clams are the longest-lived animals on the planet!

Quahogs are the longest-lived of all animals.

What Ocean Creature has the GREATEST ABILITY TO REGENERATE?

Sponges

Sponges can regenerate (re-grow) from a piece of tissue as small as the head of a pin!

There are more than 5,000 different species of sponges in the world's oceans.

NOTEPAD

Sponges can range in size from just a few centimeters or inches to several feet in diameter. To test various sponges' ability to regenerate, scientists have pressed sponges through fine mesh cloth, which separated the animal into many tiny pieces. When put back in water, the pieces actually arranged themselves to form a new sponge! If just one sponge cell breaks off by itself, it is eventually able to grow a new body on its own.

What's the HEAVIEST CRUSTACEAN?

The Atlantic Lobster

An adult Atlantic lobster can weigh more than 20 pounds (9.1 kg)!

NOTEPAD

This jumbo crustacean is found mostly on the ocean bottom near the shores of the Atlantic Ocean. It can grow up to 2 feet (.6 m) in length—with large, powerful claws that are almost as long as its body. The Atlantic lobster is the most popular food lobster for humans. U.S. and Canadian fishers catch about 80 million pounds (36 million kg) of these lobsters each year. An Atlantic lobster can live up to 15 years.

Atlantic lobsters are the most popular food lobsters for humans.

What's the Ocean Creature That TRAVELS THE FARTHEST?

The European Eel

European eels will spend about 6 months traveling nearly 4,000 miles (6,437 km) in order to lay their eggs in the ocean.

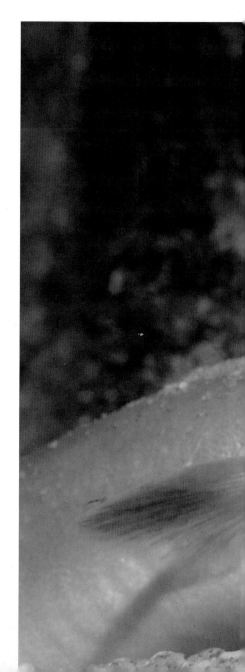

European eels spend part of their lives in freshwater and part in saltwater.

NOTEPAD

European eels live in freshwater, but they spawn (lay their eggs) in the ocean. When they are ready to spawn, these eels journey out of their river toward saltwater. To do this, they use the strong current of the Gulf Stream. Once they reach the ocean, they swim to the Sargasso Sea to lay their eggs. When the eggs hatch, the larvae drift back to the Gulf Stream, travel to the mouth of the river from which their parents came, swim upstream, and grow up in freshwater.

What's the Fish That LAYS THE MOST EGGS?

The Ocean Sunfish

In one spawning, some ocean sunfish will lay more than 30 million eggs!

The ocean sunfish is also called the mola or the headfish.

NOTEPAD

The huge ocean sunfish is also known as the mola or the headfish. It can be found mostly in tropical waters, out in the open ocean. Its body is flattened from side to side, with a small mouth and beaklike teeth. Some ocean sunfish can grow to a length of 11 feet (3.3 m) and can weigh more than 4,000 pounds (1,800 kg)! This animal is unique because—unlike most fish—the ocean sunfish does not have scales.

Which Fish Is the MOST FEROCIOUS?

The Piranha

A school of piranha can reduce a cow to a skeleton in a matter of minutes!

NOTEPAD

These ferocious meat-eating fish are found in the rivers of South America. Piranha like to travel in schools, and have excellent senses of smell and hearing. They can detect vibrations in water from great distances and are particularly attracted to the smell of blood or the struggling of a wounded animal. Strong jaws and razor-sharp teeth make them one of the most dangerous predators in freshwater.

Schools of piranha, with their razor-sharp teeth, are some of the most dangerous predators in freshwater.

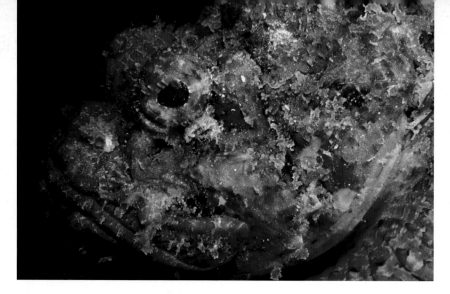

Which Fish Is the MOST VENOMOUS?

The Stonefish

This fish has enough venom to kill 12 to14 humans!

The stonefish is well named. Lying motionless on the ocean floor, it looks just like a stone. Found mostly in the Great Barrier Reef of Australia, the stonefish has an effective strategy for hunting. It is both hard to see and highly dangerous. Under its wart-covered skin, are 12 to 14 spines filled with powerful poison. If an animal touches one of these sharp spines, venom will fill the puncture, causing great pain and possibly death.

Lying motionless on the ocean floor, the venomous stonefish looks just like a coral-covered rock.

Glossary

Aborigines—one of the native peoples of Australia who have lived there since before the Europeans arrived.

Camouflage—coloring or covering that makes animals, people, and objects look like their surroundings.

Crustacean—a sea creature that has an outer skeleton.

Edible—something that can be eaten.

Embryo—a living thing that is in its first stage of development.

Hatch—when a baby animal breaks out of its egg.

Incubate—to keep eggs warm before they hatch.

Plankton—tiny animals and plants that float in oceans and lakes.

Prey—an animal that is hunted by another animal for food.

Puncture—a hole made by something sharp.

Upstream—toward the beginning of a stream.

For More Information

Books

Fine, John Christopher. *Big Stuff in the Ocean*. Golden, CO: Fulcrum Publishing, 1998.

McAuliffe, Emily. *Piranhas* (Dangerous Animals Series). Danbury, CT: Franklin Watts, Inc., 1997.

McLeish, Ewan. *Oceans and Seas* (Habitats). New York, NY: Thomson Learning, 1996.

Parker, Steve. *Eyewitness: Fish* (Dorling Kindersley Eyewitness Books). New York, NY: Dorling Kindersley, 2000.

Web Sites

Mystic Aquarium
This web site provides information on underwater life and has a special kids' section—
www.mysticaquarium.org.

OceanLink
Learn about ocean life and explore the worlds of sharks, whales, and other marine life—
www.oceanlink.island.net.

Index